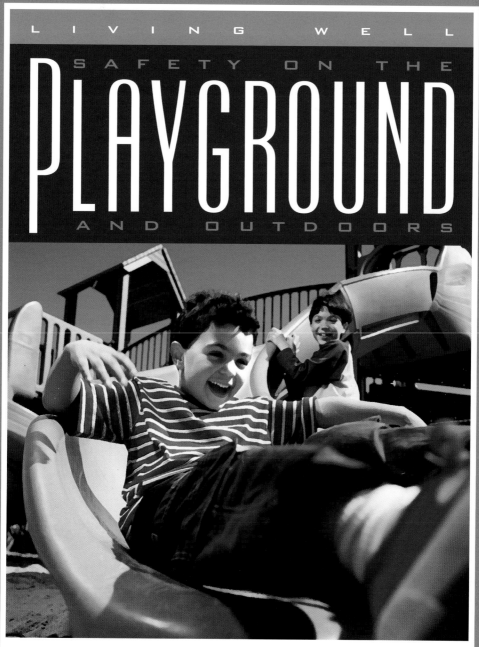

LIVING WELL

SAFETY ON THE

PLAYGROUND

AND OUTDOORS

by Lucia Raatma

THE CHILD'S WORLD®
CHANHASSEN, MINNESOTA

Published in the United States of America by The Child's World®
PO Box 326, Chanhassen, MN 55317-0326
800-599-READ
www.childsworld.com

Content Adviser:
Bridget Clementi,
Safe Kids Coordinator,
Children's Health
Education Center,
Milwaukee, Wisconsin

Photo Credits: Cover/frontispiece: Cover: Getty Images/Photodisc/Ryan McVay; cover corner: Getty Images/Photodisc/Rob Casey. Interior: Corbis: 6 (Kennan Ward), 8 (Tony Demin), 14 (William Gottlieb), 18 (LWA-Dann Tardif), 21 (Randy Faris), 24 (Mark A. Johnson), 26, 27 (Lowell Georgia), 31 (Bruce Burkhardt); Getty Images/Photodisc: 17; Getty Images/Taxi: 19 (Adam Smith), 22 (Ron Chapple); PhotoEdit: 10 (Bill Aron), 20 (Myrleen Ferguson Cate); PictureQuest: 5 (Photodisc/Andersen-Ross), 7 (Stockbyte), 9 (Edward Burchard/Index Stock Imagery), 11 (SuperStock), 12 (Philip & Karen Smith/ImageState), 13 (Bob Daemmrich/Stock, Boston Inc.), 15 (Lynne Siler/Focus Group), 16 (Phoebe Dunn/Stock Connection), 25 (David Barber/PhotoEdit).

The Child's World®: Mary Berendes, Publishing Director

Editorial Directions, Inc.: E. Russell Primm, Editorial Director; Katie Marsico, Line Editor; Matt Messbarger, Editorial Assistant; Susan Hindman, Copy Editor; Sarah E. De Capua, Proofreader; Katherine Trickle and Stephen Carl Wender, Fact Checkers; Tim Griffin/IndexServ, Indexer; Cian Loughlin O'Day, Photo Researcher; Linda S. Koutris, Photo Selector

The Design Lab: Kathleen Petelinsek, Design; Kari Thornborough, Page Production

Library of Congress Cataloging-in-Publication Data
Raatma, Lucia.
 Safety on the playground and outdoors / by Lucia Raatma.
   v. cm. — (Living well (series))
 Includes bibliographical references and index.
 Contents: A good day for a hike—Checking the weather—Camping out—At the playground—At the beach or pool—Playing it safe—Glossary—Questions and answers about safety on the playground and outdoors—Helping a friend learn about safety on the playground and outdoors—Did you know?—How to learn more about safety on the playground and outdoors.
 ISBN 1-59296-243-2 (library bound : alk. paper) 1. Playgrounds—Safety measures—Juvenile literature. [1. Outdoor recreation—Safety measures. 2. Playgrounds—Safety measures. 3. Safety.] I. Title. II. Living well (Child's World (Firm))
 GV424.R23 2005
 796'.06'8—dc22
                                                  2003027211

TABLE OF CONTENTS

CHAPTER ONE

A Good Day
for a Hike

On a warm spring day, Emily bounded out of bed. She and her scout troop were going for a hike, and she could hardly wait. She looked out the window, and the sky looked clear. But Emily wanted to be sure, so she turned on the radio to hear about the weather. The **forecast** was "sunny, with a high in the 70s." Perfect. She dressed in light cotton clothes and made sure not to wear scented lotion—the smell would attract bugs. She tied back her hair in a ponytail, slipped on a baseball cap, and laced up her sturdy waterproof boots.

Once downstairs, she filled up her backpack. She put in a **canteen** of water, a **compass,** a whistle, a flashlight, a sandwich, some nuts and raisins, and a bottle of sunscreen.

By the time Emily heard her friend's car outside, she was packed and ready for her hiking trip. It's important to be prepared if you plan on spending the day outdoors. This way, you can stay safe and have a good time.

Sunscreen is a lotion containing chemicals that can protect you from the sun's rays. Emily had already put on a layer of the sunscreen, but she'd need to add more later. She also packed an extra pair of shorts, socks, and a shirt—just in case.

She ate a quick breakfast and then a horn sounded outside. Emily knew the gang was there to pick her up. "Bye, Mom," she said. "We'll be back by dinner."

"Have fun, sweetheart," her mother answered. "And watch out for bears." They both laughed.

You probably won't end up face to face with any bears if you go hiking, but you should still be careful! Try to avoid spots where bears have been seen in the past and make sure an adult goes with you if you plan on being in a wilderness area.

Emily doubted that she would run into any bears that day, but who could be sure? As she walked out of her house, she felt ready for anything.

Being prepared is one great way to stay safe outdoors. You can never predict what may happen on a hike or even on a day at the beach, so it is a good idea to be ready for all kinds of **emergencies.** The weather

may change, someone could get hurt, or a piece of equipment could

break. Some say the best rule for staying safe outdoors is to expect

the unexpected.

Weather conditions can change unexpectedly, so pack clothes or supplies that will help you stay warm and dry if you encounter a storm.

CHAPTER TWO

CHECKING
THE WEATHER

It is fun to spend time outdoors. Skiing and cycling, boating and

playing ball are all great activities. But before you head outside, it

is important to consider the weather.

*Skiing is a fun outdoor activity—just check the weather forecast to make
sure you won't be hitting the slopes in the middle of a snowstorm!*

Bad weather can be a problem for many outdoor events. A rainstorm can take all the pleasure out of a picnic. But worse, lightning and heavy winds can cause serious **injuries.** So

Do not stand under trees during a thunderstorm. If you can, seek indoor shelter and don't go back outside until the storm has passed.

always check the weather forecast before you make outdoor plans.

If you are already outside and you hear thunder, try to seek shelter, or someplace where you can stay protected from the bad weather. Thunder means lightning is close by. Do not stand under trees, since trees and other tall objects are usually among the first things to get struck by lightning. Instead, get inside a building, a car, or a cave. Avoid holding metal items or standing in or near water during a thunderstorm. Metal and water conduct the electrical currents that are created when lightning strikes. If you are struck by lightning, you could be hurt or even killed.

Extreme heat and extreme cold are also problems. In hot weather, drink plenty of water and use sunscreen. If you get too hot, seek shelter in the shade or in an air-conditioned building. When it is very cold, you can suffer from **frostbite** or **hypothermia.** So cover as much skin as you can with gloves, scarves, a hat, a parka, and other clothing. Dress in layers so you'll be prepared if the weather changes.

Always be sure to pack water when you go on an outdoor trip.

CHAPTER THREE

CAMPING OUT

Have you ever gone camping with your family or friends? You probably enjoyed sitting around the fire and telling stories. Perhaps you found sleeping in a tent to be a little scary. But there is nothing to be scared about. If you take certain steps ahead of time, you're doing your best to be safe.

Camping is a popular outdoor activity that you can enjoy with your family. Careful planning ahead of time will make your trip fun, comfortable, and safe.

Be sure to pack a **first-aid**

kit in case anyone gets hurt.

Insect bites and minor cuts can

be easily treated at the campsite.

For more serious injuries, you

will need to seek medical help.

So always pack a two-way radio

or cell phone. Other supplies

you should include are a map,

compass, flashlight, insect spray,

*A map and compass will come in handy
if you get lost in the wilderness.*

tools to help you start a fire, and a variety of clothes.

Before you set up your tent, choose a level spot. Avoid areas that

have poison ivy, anthills, bees, and other dangers. Also try to avoid

areas where there are plants that produce fruit or berries—wild animals might travel to these places in search of food. Position your tent far

enough away from the fire that a spark cannot reach it. Once you

have started a fire, make sure someone watches it at all times. During

certain seasons, forest fires can spread easily. If it is dry or windy

outside, consider using a portable stove instead of building a fire.

Respect the wildlife around you. Do not leave out food that

may attract bears, insects, and other animals. Store food in sealed

Be careful when building your campfire. Make sure that you never leave it unattended.

Bringing a flashlight along on a camping trip will help scare away any animals that might wander near your campsite at night.

containers that are kept away from your tent. Avoid wearing scented lotions because these also may attract insects and animals. At night, keep a flashlight nearby—most animals will be scared off by the light.

During your campout, you might enjoy meeting other people who are camp-ing, too. But be sure to always stay with the adults you came with. They are in charge of your safety. And you may not be able to trust all of the strangers you meet.

When you are ready to pack up and leave the wilderness, be sure to clean up your campsite. Take all of your supplies with you. And throw away your garbage in the proper place. You want to leave the campsite clean for the next people who use it. Be sure your campfire is completely out. Drown the fire with water, and make certain that all the branches, coals, and **embers** are wet. Forest fires can start from just a single spark.

Don't forget to make sure your campfire is completely out before you leave. Forest fires are incredibly destructive and often result from careless campers.

What If You Get Lost?

You have probably seen all sorts of rescue stories on television—tales of people being lost on mountainsides and then being saved. These stories may sound both exciting and scary. But in reality, do you know what to do if you get lost outdoors and you don't have a two-way radio or cell phone?

If you are hiking or skiing and get separated from your group, some say the best advice is to stay put. If you walk back and forth, it may be harder for people to find you. But at the same time, you want to be easily seen. So it makes sense an open space. If you are able to move to such an area, stay put once you get there.

Try to make yourself visible. Blow a whistle if you have one. Display any brightly colored item you might have with you. Use matches or other tools to start a fire, but first be sure to build a protective ring of stones or rocks around where your fire will be. Also, if it is very windy, be careful and consider doing something else to draw attention to yourself. Above all, try not to panic. Keep yourself safe while you wait for

CHAPTER FOUR

AT THE PLAYGROUND

There are probably playgrounds in your neighborhood and at your school. Before you play, be sure all the equipment is in good shape. Broken swings or rusty climbing bars are dangerous, or likely to cause harm. If your playground equipment is in need of repair, talk to an adult about ways to improve it.

Old and rusty swings such as this one can be dangerous if they are not replaced or repaired.

You might enjoy climbing on the monkey bars at the playground. Just be sure to hang on tightly and move slowly so you don't fall.

The surface of the playground should be rubber or wood chips. Avoid concrete and rough sand because falling on these surfaces can hurt you. Take special care when you are climbing on playground equipment. Go slowly and hang on tightly. If the bars are wet, stay off the equipment until it dries.

When you are playing, be sure to watch out for other kids. Do not walk right in front or in back of the swings, because the person swinging could accidentally hit you. Be sure to always sit—and not stand or kneel—on the swings. Take turns on slides and don't push anyone up the steps. And never climb up a slide. Kids sliding down might crash into you and everyone could get hurt. Also check to make sure no one is playing near the bottom of the slide, and always slide down feet first.

Look before you slide! You don't want to accidentally hit any kids that might be standing near the bottom.

If you are enjoying other sports at the playground, follow the rules for those sports. When in-line skating, be sure to wear elbow and knee pads, as well as a helmet. These will protect you if you have an

accident. Steer clear of other kids—especially little ones—who

might not be able to get out of your way quickly. When biking, wear

a helmet and try to travel on bike paths. If there are no special paths

for bikers in your neighborhood, ride in areas where you won't risk

hitting people who are

out for a walk or a jog.

When you and

your friends play team

sports, follow the rules

of good sportsmanship.

Play fair and never

cheat. Don't try to hurt

other players just so your

If these two skaters fall, they'll be less likely to get hurt since they're wearing protective knee pads and helmets.

Members of opposite teams often shake hands after a game is over. Even if you're on the losing team, it's still important to show good sportsmanship.

team can win. Playing the game should be fun, and hurting others

takes the fun out of it for everyone. If anyone does get injured,

find an adult right away.

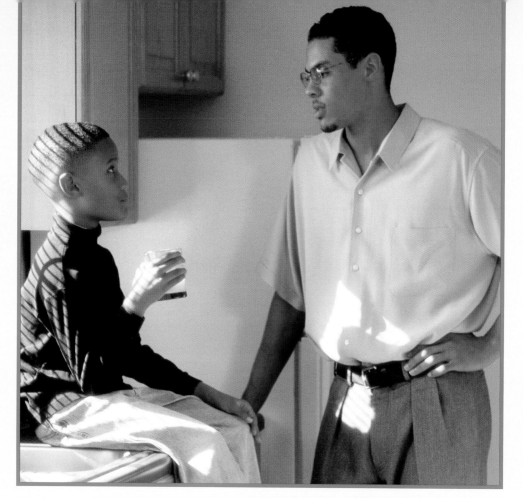

Talk to your parents or another trusted adult about what you should do if a stranger approaches you on the playground.

Be careful of strangers who might hang around the playground. Some strangers might try to trick you or hurt you. If anyone you don't know offers you money, candy, or a ride, run away as quickly as you can. Tell a trusted adult about the stranger and ask for help.

CHAPTER FIVE

AT THE BEACH
OR POOL

Being a strong swimmer is one of the best ways to stay safe at the beach or pool. If you don't know how to swim, talk to your parents about taking lessons. The more experience you have swimming, the safer you will be.

When you go out in a boat, always wear a life jacket. A life jacket could help you stay afloat if your boat turns over.

Never swim alone. Always have a buddy go with you so you can look out for each other. And swim only when there is a lifeguard present. If you get into trouble, try your best to stay calm until a lifeguard can reach you.

At the beach, check the surf conditions before you get in the water. Strong waves or currents can be dangerous. If there are warning signs or flags posted, pay attention to them. If it is unsafe to swim, stay out of the water! And always respect the animals and plants that are in the water with you. Avoid patches of underwater plants, because you might get caught in them. And stay far away from sea jellies, rays, and other sea animals. Their stings can hurt you. If you ever see a shark, get out of the water as calmly as you can and tell a lifeguard right away.

If you ever get in trouble while swimming, call for a lifeguard. And always ask a lifeguard for help if someone in your group is missing. Life-guards are trained to assist you and to keep you safe.

If you are swimming in the ocean and notice sea jellies floating nearby, get out of the water or try to avoid swimming near them.

CHAPTER SIX

PLAYING IT SAFE

Most of the time, being outdoors is fun. And you probably don't run into trouble often. But when you do, it's best to be prepared for it. One way is to learn first aid and other life-saving treatments at your local Red Cross office or hospital. You can also learn more about wilderness safety from the Boy Scouts and Girl Scouts. Make the decision to be safe when you are outdoors.

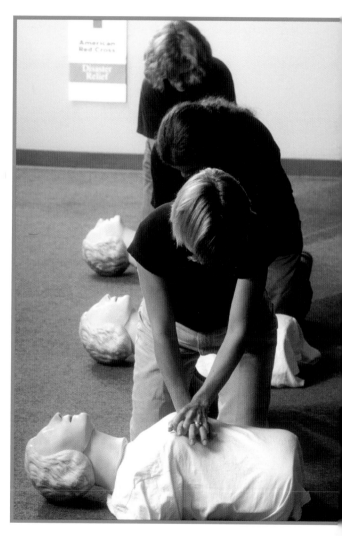

These people are practicing a life-saving treatment on dummies at a first-aid class. First-aid classes will prepare you to handle a variety of emergency situations, including those that might happen outdoors.

Sunburns can be painful. They take all the fun out of a day at

the beach or park! So avoid spending hours and hours in the sun.

Occasionally take shelter under an umbrella, or put on a big hat and

a long-sleeved shirt if you plan to stay out long. Too much time

in the sun can lead to a burn—and possibly even to skin **cancer.**

Beach umbrellas will protect you from the strong rays of the sun. But even
if you have a beach umbrella, don't forget to use your sunscreen!

Avoiding Sunburn

Some people think there is nothing better than a deep, dark tan. But the truth is that the sun can be dangerous for your skin. Though we get Vitamin D and other benefits from small doses of sunshine, spending long periods of time in the sun is not a good idea. The most dangerous times are from 10 A.M. to 2 P.M.

Whenever you are outside, be sure to wear sunscreen. You should apply the sunscreen every two hours or so, and always reapply it after swimming. Use sunscreen even on overcast days, since you can still get burned when it's cloudy. Also, be sure to wear sunglasses, which will protect your eyes from the sun.

Glossary

accident (AK-si-duhnt) An accident is an event that takes place unexpectedly and often involves people being hurt.

cancer (KAN-sur) Cancer is a serious disease that involves some cells growing faster than others. These cells then destroy healthy organs and tissues.

canteen (kan-TEEN) A canteen is a portable container that holds water.

compass (KUHM-puhss) A compass is an instrument used for finding directions. Its magnetic needle always points north.

embers (EM-burz) Embers are the hot, glowing remains of a fire.

emergencies (i-MUR-juhn-seez) Emergencies are sudden and dangerous situations that require immediate attention.

first-aid (furst-ayd) First-aid describes the care given to someone who is sick or hurt before he or she sees a doctor.

forecast (FOR-kast) A forecast is the prediction of something that will happen in the future. A weather forecast predicts the weather for the coming days.

frostbite (FRAWST-bite) Frostbite is a dangerous physical condition caused by very cold weather. Frostbite damages fingers, toes, ears, and other parts of the body.

hypothermia (hye-puh-THUR-mee-uh) Hypothermia is a condition in which a person's body temperature is dangerously low.

injuries (IN-juh-reez) An injury is a condition of damage or harm.

Questions and Answers about Safety on the Playground and Outdoors

I've heard that if you see a bear, the best thing to do is to play dead. Is that right? Not necessarily. It is hard to tell how a bear will react to humans. Before your next camping trip, ask the local park rangers about any bears in the area and what you should do if you see them. The best advice is to avoid them altogether. Keep food in sealed containers and hang it from the branch of a tree, out of the reach of bears. Don't go hiking alone, and be aware of your surroundings at all times.

Some older kids hang around the playground where we play sports. Sometimes they offer us stuff they say will help us have a good time. What are they talking about? They are probably talking about drugs, and you should ignore them. Drugs never helped anyone have a good time in the long run. Talk to your parents or another trusted adult about these kids right away. You may even want to call the police.

The playground in my neighborhood is falling apart. Is there anything I can do? Sure. Call your local police department right away and report the problem. Or ask your parents to speak with elected officials or a neighborhood volunteer group about the playground. Volunteer groups can sometimes work with city officials to raise money for repairs and new equipment. You could be part of this effort, too!

I'm not a great swimmer, but if I have a raft, I can still go in deep water, right? Don't be so sure! Rafts are fun, but you should never expect them to keep you afloat. Work on becoming a stronger swimmer. Talk to your parents about taking lessons to help you get better.

Helping a Friend Learn about Safety on the Playground and Outdoors

▸ Ask your friend to take a first-aid course with you. That way, you can help each other be prepared for outdoor emergencies.

▸ Talk to your friend about organizing a group to go camping. Ask some adults to come along. You can all work together to learn about camping safety.

▸ Be a buddy. You and your friend can go swimming and hiking together. You will be safer if you stick with each other.

Did You Know?

▸ When lightning strikes a tree, electricity runs down the trunk, through the roots, and into the ground around it. So never stand under a tree during a thunderstorm.

▸ Most playground accidents involve falls—often with injuries to a child's face or head.

▸ You should never kid around in the water and yell for help when you don't need it. Lifeguards need to help those in trouble, so never waste their time with a joke.

How to Learn More about
Safety on the Playground and Outdoors

At the Library

Allen, Missy. *Dangerous Sports*. Broomall, Pa.: Chelsea House, 1993.

Boelts, Maribeth. *A Kid's Guide to Staying Safe around Water*.
New York: PowerKids Press, 1997.

Chaiet, Donna, and Francine Russell. *The Safe Zone:*
A Kid's Guide to Personal Safety. New York: Beech Tree, 1998.

Gutman, Bill. *Recreation Can Be Risky*. New York: Twenty First Century Books, 1996.

Hayhurst, Chris. *Bike Trekking: Have Fun, Be Smart*.
New York: Rosen Publishing Group, 2000.

Sanders, Pete. *Personal Safety*. Brookfield, Conn.: Millbrook Press, 1998.

Whitefeather, Willy. *Willy Whitefeather's Outdoor Survival Handbook*.
Niwot, Colo.: Roberts Rhinehart, 2000.

On the Web

Visit our home page for lots of links about safety on the playground and outdoors:
http://www.childsworld.com/links.html

Note to Parents, Teachers, and Librarians: We routinely verify our
Web links to make sure they're safe, active sites—so encourage your
readers to check them out!

Through the Mail or by Phone

American Red Cross National Headquarters
431 18th Street NW
Washington, DC 20006
202/303-4498

National SAFE KIDS Campaign
1301 Pennsylvania Avenue NW
Suite 100
Washington, DC 20004
202/662-0600

The Nemours Center for Children's Health Media
Alfred I. duPont Hospital for Children
1600 Rockland Road
Wilmington, DE 19803
302/651-4046

Survive Outdoors, Inc.
1643 North Alpine Road
Suite 104, PMB #105
Rockford, IL 61107
815/623-7749

Index

About the Author

Lucia Raatma received her bachelor's degree in English literature from the University of South Carolina and her master's degree in cinema studies from New York University. She has written a wide range of books for young people. When she is not researching or writing, she enjoys going to movies, practicing yoga, and spending time with her family. She lives in New York.